How To...

INCLUDES ONLINE VIDEO LESSONS WITH DEMONSTRATIONS OF ALL THE PLAYING EXAMPLES IN THE BOOK

PLAY BOOGIE WO GUITAR

BY DAVE RUBIN

To access video visit:
www.halleonard.com/mylibrary

Enter Code
8105-3991-7491-0069

ISBN 978-1-4950-6053-3

HAL•LEONARD®

7777 W. BLUEMOUND RD. P.O. BOX 13819 MILWAUKEE, WI 53213

In Australia Contact:
Hal Leonard Australia Pty. Ltd.
4 Lentara Court
Cheltenham, Victoria, 3192 Australia
Email: ausadmin@halleonard.com.au

Visit Hal Leonard Online at
www.halleonard.com

CONTENTS

DEDICATION AND ACKNOWLEDGMENTS

I would like to dedicate this book to the memory of Rommie Telfair. Thanks to David Cudaback for his invaluable research and friendship.

PREFACE

Boogie woogie music is one of the greatest influences on the blues, swing jazz, and rock 'n' roll. The style is usually identified more with the piano than the guitar, especially following the prewar and WWII craze as epitomized by Meade Lux Lewis, Pete Johnson, and Albert Ammons—the literal "Big Three" masters of the "walking 88s." However, boogie woogie actually seems to have originated with guitar players during the latter half of the 19th century in the rough "barrel houses" of the turpentine and lumber camps of the American South.

Novelist, folklorist, and anthropologist Zora Neale Hurston described it as such:

"One guitar was enough for a dance. To have two was considered excellent. Where two were playing, one man played the lead, and the other seconded him. The first player was 'picking,' and the second was 'framming,'—that is, playing chords while the lead carried the melody by dexterous finger work. Sometimes a third player was added, and he played a tom-tom effect on the lower strings."

"Dexterous finger work" indeed! Given the often muscular tempos at which boogie woogie is played, a certain amount of dexterous chops are required. The mission of this book is to provide them and all the necessary aspects of technique and style in order to play this house-rocking guitar music.

The lessons are arranged to lead incrementally and logically from the foundational elements to the last chapter, where the ultimate awaits for guitarists: improvising within a variety of classic boogie woogie accompaniment patterns.

Editor's note: Although all of the examples on the video are performed fingerstyle, picking directions are given throughout for those who wish to use a pick instead.

– *Dave Rubin*
NYC

ABOUT THE VIDEO

Every music figure in this book includes a matching video with an explanation and demonstration by author Dave Rubin. To access the videos, simply visit **www.halleonard.com/mylibrary** and enter the code found on page 1 of this book. From here, you can download or stream all of the video files.

HISTORY OF BOOGIE WOOGIE GUITAR

THE EARLY YEARS

The first recorded guitar boogie bass-string patterns appeared on "Lead Pencil Blues" by Johnny Temple in 1935. A year later, Robert Johnson waxed the landmark guitar boogie blues "Sweet Home Chicago"—a classic of enormous influence. The boogie patterns appearing in both became known as "cut boogie" because they involved the 5th and 6th (and sometimes ♭7th) degrees of the Mixolydian mode, but not the tonality-defining major 3rd regularly utilized in piano boogie woogie. "I'm a Steady Rollin' Man" and "Stop Breakin' Down," both recorded by Johnson in 1937 in abbreviated cut-boogie form, represent his last examples of the form. In time, blues guitarists would regularly combine the critical ♭3rd "blues note" in conjunction with the major 3rd in bass-string riffs Johnson helped popularize.

Boogie woogie guitar also developed among country musicians. Johnny Barfield recorded the loping "Boogie Woogie" in 1939 as the first country boogie. He based it on the landmark piano classic "Pinetop's Boogie Woogie," which was recorded in 1928 but famously heard at Carnegie Hall in 1939 at John Hammond Sr.'s genre-busting *From Spirituals to Swing* concert. Boogie woogie guitar would become a notable subgenre of country music as the pioneering Delmore Brothers, among others, recorded numerous "boogies," including "Freight Train Boogie" and "Hillbilly Boogie" in 1946 and "Mobile Boogie" a year later. It should be stated, however, that not all songs with "boogie" in the title are truly based on boogie woogie techniques.

THE 1940s

"Hillbilly Boogie," in particular, sounds remarkably like one of the undisputed postwar classics of guitar boogie woogie, the eponymous "Guitar Boogie" by the underappreciated Arthur "Guitar Boogie" Smith (1921–2014). Smith, who played banjo and fiddle as well as guitar, originally recorded and released it to regional success on a small label in 1945, when it was subsequently purchased by a larger label and re-released in 1948. Smith boogied on a Martin D-27 flat-top acoustic—not an electric as is often mistakenly thought. The infectious track would go on to make the *Billboard* Pop chart and the Country chart, where it was the first instrumental to do so, while reputedly selling three million copies worldwide. Though his commercial star would not rise again until 1963, he composed over 500 songs, including "Feudin' Banjos" in 1955, which became the "Dueling Banjos" theme song in the 1973 movie *Deliverance*. The resulting copyright infringement case was settled in his favor.

The same year "Guitar Boogie" was strutting up the pop and country charts, "Boogie Chillun" (or "Chillen") by John Lee Hooker appeared seemingly out of nowhere in a blues paradigm shift. Perhaps only Garfield Akers' "Cottonfield Blues" (1929) bears any previous resemblance at all. It would hit #1 on the R&B charts in 1949 as the first electric blues to do so, sell one million copies, and become the basis of countless blues and rock songs down to the present day, including the similar "Bad Dog" (1953) by Boogie Bill Webb. Essentially a I-chord vamp, the hard driving, swinging shuffle beat of "Boogie Chillun" is boogie woogie guitar at its most elemental and powerful.

If anyone could be seen to successfully take off on Hooker's example, it would be Dr. Isaiah "Ike" Ross, the one-man band of boogie and blues. His recording career began in Memphis in 1951 with "Boogie Disease" (1952), which featured him on vocals, harmonica, and guitar (with an accompanying drummer) and became his signature tune. His "Mississippi Blues," originally titled "Cat Squirrel" (1953), was covered by Cream on their debut, *Fresh Cream* (1966).

THE 1950s

Concurrently, jump blues performed by small ensembles, as opposed to the larger swing bands of the earlier era, was beginning to grow in popularity. Walking boogie bass lines on the upright bass or piano grooved the energy while bleating and honking saxophones held sway over electric guitars for the most part until the genre, with generous helpings from swing jazz and country music, morphed into rock 'n' roll. A major exception is "Rocket 88" (1951), a raucous, groundbreaking jump blues by Jackie Brenston and his Delta Cats, powered by Willie Kizart's distorted electric guitar, which hit #1 on the R&B charts and is, in the eyes of many, the first rock 'n' roll song. Another exception is the raucous "Hello Little Boy" (1953) by Ruth Brown with the legendary Mickey "Guitar" Baker "walking" his axe in unison with the bass.

A blues guitar immortal who had inserted deftly picked boogie lines into his late 1940s and early 1950s songs was Gatemouth Brown. "Atomic Energy" (1949) lives up to its title, while "Boogie Rambler" (1949) opens with a classic walking boogie guitar line. "Boogie Uproar" (1953) features Gate opening with a pumping, inventive line, and "You Got Money" (1953) finds him adding shuffling eighth-note boogie propulsion to the verses in conjunction with the steady walking quarter notes of the acoustic bass. On the "other side of the tracks," the C&W folk were still getting down, too. Of postwar importance was Tennessee Ernie Ford with "The Shotgun Boogie" (1950) featuring the dynamic picking of Jimmy Bryant and steel guitarist Speedy West, in addition to Merrill Moore on his "Big Bug Boogie" and "Blueberry Boogie" (1953).

Blues legend Eddie "Guitar Slim" Jones, renowned for his raw distortion, exceptional showmanship, and his slow blues classic "The Things I Used to Do" (1953), cut a few boogie-based tracks, including "Guitar Slim" the same year and "Quicksand" (1955). By this time, rock 'n' roll was the "baby" of the blues, and early examples in the mid-to-late 1950s grabbed on to pumping guitar boogie patterns to intensify the lust inherent in the music. The outrageously talented Little Richard played rocking boogie woogie piano while also incorporating guitar/bass boogie lines into his classics "Lucille" (1957) and "Good Golly Miss Molly" (1958).

The year 1955 was a watershed moment for guitar rock 'n' roll, with none other than Bo Diddley bridging blues and rock with his classic monochord boogie "I'm a Man," derived from Muddy Waters' "Mannish Boy." Typically, however, cut-boogie patterns were utilized, and no more so than in the epochal music of our "Father," Chuck Berry. Though "Maybelline" sports a two-beat country rhythm, many of his subsequent hits were based on the cut boogie, including "Roll Over, Beethoven" (1956), "School Day" (1957), "Rock and Roll Music" (1957), "Sweet Little Sixteen" b/w "Reelin' and Rocking" (1958), "Johnny B. Goode" b/w "Around and Around" (1958), "Carol" (1958), "Sweet Little Rock and Roller" (1958), "Little Queenie" (1959), "Back in the U.S.A." (1959), "Memphis, Tennessee" (1959), and "No Particular Place to Go" (1964). The titanic Fats Domino in New Orleans broke nationally in 1955 with the boogie-powered "Ain't That a Shame," followed by "Blue Monday" (1956) and "I'm Walkin'" (1957). The "King," crucially supported by the late rock 'n' roll guitar pioneer Scotty Moore, boogied with "Don't Be Cruel" (1956), "Hound Dog" (1956), "Too Much" (1957), "Jailhouse Rock" (1957), "I Got Stung" (1958), and the stomping "Hard-Headed Woman" (1958) from the soundtrack of *King Creole*. Teen idol Ricky (later "Rick") Nelson performed a credible version of Domino's "I'm Walkin'" (1957), debuting it and his singing career on his parents' TV show when he was 16. He also added his polite take on the boogie with "Believe What You Say" (1958), featuring the country rock legend James Burton burning on lead guitar. "Doghouse" bassist Bill Black, who helped "invent" rock 'n' roll with Elvis, went on to form a swinging, boogie shuffle instrumental combo while producing the R&B hit "Smokie Pt. 2" (1959).

The late 1950s saw an increase in popularity of instrumental rock 'n' roll records, many of which are prominently guitar boogie-driven. Bill Doggett's "Honky Tonk (Pts. 1 & 2)," with illustrious jazzy blues guitarist Billy Butler, was kept out of the #1 chart position by "Heartbreak Hotel" in 1956. And 1959 was one of the peak instrumental years, with "Bongo Rock" by percussionist Preston Epps, the Virtues' "Guitar Boogie Shuffle" (a cover of "Guitar Boogie"), "The Happy Organ" by Dave "Baby" Cortez featuring blues guitarist Wild Jimmy Spruill, the Rock-A-Teens' silly "Woo-Hoo," and "Red River Rock" by Johnny & The Hurricanes. The latter had many other hits with guitarist Dave Yorko, including "Beatnik Fly" (1960). The rockabilly cats of the late 1950s were also boogie fans as heard on Johnny Bond's classic "Hot Rod Lincoln" (1960), the same year as a boogie cover of Jimmie Rodgers' "Muleskinner Blues" by the presciently named Fendermen. Curiously, Duane Eddy, the arguable "Twang King" of instrumental guitar, did not proffer many boogie lines except later on in "(Dance with the) Guitar Man" (1962), "Hard Times" (featuring the country rock virtuoso and pioneer James Burton, 1966), and "Roadhouse Boogie" (1982) with Ry Cooder on slide guitar.

On the country side, both Jimmy Bryant and Joe Maphis—two of the hottest pickers to ever blister the strings—incorporated boogie woogie concepts into their genre, often with spectacular results. "Stratosphere Boogie" (1954), by the former, and "Flying Fingers" (1957), from the latter, are just two examples worth seeking out.

THE 1960s

The early 1960s brought a host of other late, lamented classics, such as "Bumble Boogie" (1961) by the studio band B. Bumble and the Stingers, featuring ace session guitarist Tommy Tedesco, and their "Nut Rocker" (1962) with the unsung guitar hero Rene Hall. An instrumental version of Chuck Berry's "Memphis" (1963) by the late blues-rock virtuoso Lonnie Mack became a must-learn for budding blues and rock guitarists. The blues was exceptionally represented instrumentally by the unsurpassed Texas guitar slinger Freddie King. As adept at singing as playing with passion and chops, he ran a "string" of timeless standards featuring boogie riffs, just in time for the instrumental surf music era. Beginning with the landmark "Hide Away" (1960), they included "Side Tracked" (1961), "Heads Up" (1961), "Out Front" (1961), and "Low Tide" (1963). Before the British Invasion stormed the U.S. shores, Johnny Kidd & the Pirates cut "Shakin' All Over" (1960), while the Swinging Blue Jeans followed with their hit cover of "The Hippy Hippy Shake" (1963), originally composed and played by unsung rock guitarist Chan Romero in 1959. The Yardbirds with Jeff Beck covered "I'm a Man" (1965), extending the coda into a "rave-up" for "El Becko." Wanting to show how the Beatles could be "heavy" and "bluesy" like the Rolling Stones, John Lennon provided the impetus for the boogie-derived riff in "Day Tripper" (1965).

The "rhythm" in R&B music typically made boogie riffs incompatible, though the Stax Records instrumentals "Last Night" (1961) by the Mar-Keys and "Green Onions" (1962) from Booker T. & the M.G.s are notable exceptions. Likewise, instrumental surf music circa 1962–64, while sometimes built on 12-bar blues progressions, did not, as a rule, incorporate walking bass lines. The late 1960s "Blues Revival," however, produced musicians who paid attention to the thumping big beat. Prominent were the Los Angeles band Canned Heat (formed in 1965), who based their sound, to a large extent, on the primal boogies of John Lee Hooker. Their hit single "On the Road Again" (1968) and epic album tracks like "Fried Hockey Boogie" and "Refried Boogie" (both 1968), established their identity and led to *Hooker 'n Heat* (1971), their seemingly preordained collaboration with John Lee Hooker. They continue to boogie on down to the present day, having fielded a virtual army of changing personnel.

Meanwhile, in Chicago, the magnificent blues guitarist Magic Sam gave out amazing boogie tracks like "I Feel So Good (I Wanna Boogie")" and "Lookin' Good," featured on *West Side Soul* (1967). Down in Texas, Johnny Winter recorded "Mean Town Blues" (1968), which would become one of his signature slide pieces, and Norman Greenbaum had a huge hit with "Spirit in the Sky" (1969). The Rolling Stones, of course, were no strangers to the power of the boogie, with "Parachute Woman" (1968), "Midnight Rambler" (1969), and "Rocks Off," plus the scatological "Turd on the Run" from *Exile on Main St.* (1972), among their many cut-boogie classics.

THE 1970s

The 1970s saw the T. Rex hit "Get It On (Bang a Gong)" (1971) and "La Grange" (1973), a "tribute" to John Lee Hooker by ZZ Top, bringing the boogie beat to the radio waves with the spot-on vocal imitation of "The Boogie Man" by guitarist Billy "F" Gibbons. Previously, the "Little Ol' Band from Texas" had included the cut boogie "Mushmouth Shoutin'" on *Rio Grande Mud* (1972) and would record other streamlined boogies later in their ongoing career. The irresistible basic rhythm even found its way into hit pop folk-rock tunes like "A Horse with No Name" (1972) by America. Bad Company grabbed their own hit with the classic cut-boogie rocker "Can't Get Enough" (1974), as did the post-blues version of Fleetwood Mac with "Don't Stop" (1977). Concurrently, the disco craze was picking up steam with songs containing "boogie" in the title while having no relation to the aforementioned rhythms.

Southern rock bands had their glorious moment in 1970s with boogie rhythms sometimes incorporated into their blues-based music. Curiously, the Allman Brothers did not indulge, for the most part, outside of their iconic version of Blind Willie McTell's "Statesboro Blues" (1971), while Black Oak Arkansas, Lynyrd Skynyrd, the Outlaws, Molly Hatchet, and others employed the boogie to varying degrees. Black Oak Arkansas ramped up the boogie quotient on their cover of LaVern Baker's "Jim Dandy" (1973), while Skynyrd did likewise with a cover of J.J Cale's "Call Me the Breeze" (1974) and the late Steve Gaines' original composition "I Know a Little" (1977). Though perhaps stretching the definition of boogie, the Outlaws' epic guitar rant "Green Grass and High Tides" (1975) certainly possesses the overall feel and spirit. Molly Hatchet had their biggest hit with the boogying "Flirtin' with Disaster" (1980).

George Thorogood has long been a standard-bearer for basic boogie, as well as the "Bo Diddley beat," since the mid-1970s. Included among many is a cover of Hooker's "Huckle Up, Baby" (1974), Hank Williams' "Move It On Over" (1978), and his originals "Bad to the Bone" (1982) and "I Drink Alone" (1985). Ably representing British boogie blues beginning in the 1970s, Foghat mined somewhat similar territory with a bigger, bolder sound. Their cover of Junior Parker's "Drivin' Wheel" (1976), the live version of Willie Dixon's "Just Want to Make Love to You" (1977), and their original, salacious "Slow Ride" (1975) convincingly prove the magic combination of cranked Marshall amps and grinding blues-rock!

THE 1980s AND BEYOND

Though blues guitarists kept, and will always keep, the boogie beat as a foundation of their music, the rock and pop worlds moved in different directions in the 1980s. Some well-known exceptions were "Pink Cadillac" (1984) by Bruce Springsteen, Dire Straits' "Money for Nothing" (1985), "Keep Your Hands to Yourself" (1986) from the Georgia Satellites, and "I'm the Only One" (1993) by the bluesy Melissa Etheridge. Though a bit of a stretch, Michael Jackson's "Beat It" (1982) and "Billie Jean" (1983), along with the Beastie Boys' "(You Gotta) Fight for Your Right (To Party)" (1986) qualify as boogie-based under a broad umbrella, as does the Knack's "My Sharona" (1979).

Australian acoustic guitar virtuoso Tommy Emmanuel has been recording since 1979, and his albums and live performances of jazz and pop standards always include at least one jaw-dropping solo guitar boogie played with a flatpick.

In the realm of recent pop and rock music, perhaps only the iconoclastic, blues-obsessed Jack White has even come close to the boogie beat with his popular song "Ball and Biscuit" from the White Stripes' hit album *Elephant* (2003). Given the way the blues has ceased to have any significant influence on contemporary music since the 1990s, it is no surprise. However, blues and blues-rock guitarists have boogie riffs in their DNA and will always incorporate them in one way or another. As John Lee Hooker famously stated in "Boogie Chillun," "Let that boy boogie woogie. It's in him, and it's got to come out!"

CHAPTER 1
WALKING BASS LINES: THE HEARTBEAT OF BOOGIE WOOGIE

THE MIXOLYDIAN MODE

Boogie woogie walking bass lines, often doubled on the guitar, are the heart of the music. They are derived from the Mixolydian mode (as shown in Fig. 1), the major pentatonic scale, the composite blues scale, and the blues scale. With the proliferation of dominant—seventh, ninth, or 13th—chords in the blues, the Mixolydian mode, being the "dominant" mode, is the most prominent.

Fig. 1   A Mixolydian

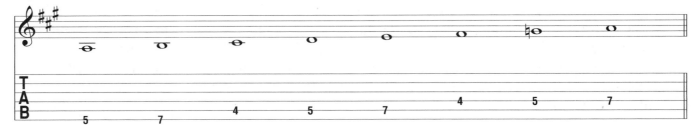

Fig. 2 shows a standard 12-bar blues in the common key of A. Containing the I (A7), IV (D7), and V (E7) chords, simple quarter-note, Mixolydian mode-derived bass lines are used, relative to each chord change, to indicate the harmony. This is critical to understanding the basic concept of boogie woogie music: the bass lines, or patterns, are virtually always relative to each chord change. In other words, we use the A Mixolydian mode for the I chord (A7), the D Mixolydian mode for the IV chord (D7), and the E Mixolydian mode for the V chord (E7). **Performance Tip:** Be aware how the bass lines are four-note truncated forms of the relative Mixolydian in order to fit within the span of one four-beat measure in 4/4 time.

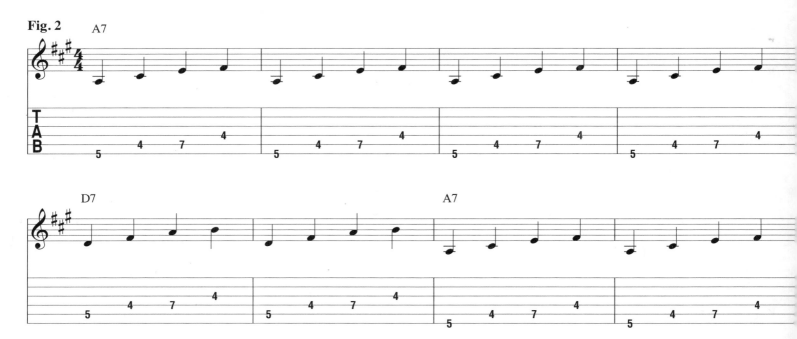

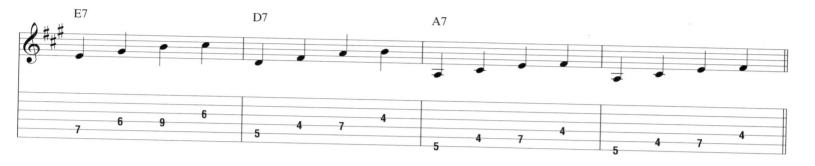

Fig. 3 contains the same bass lines as Fig. 2 but is played in more typical swinging eighth notes.
Performance Tip: Especially at quicker tempos, alternate down and up pick strokes on a riff like this.

Another common Mixolydian walking bass line, shown in Fig. 4, involves an ascending and descending eighth-note pattern utilizing every note from the key of A, save for the 2nd degree (B). Observe how the line covers two measures, necessitating cutting the phrase in half in measures 9 and 10 for the V (E7) and IV (D7) chords, respectively. Alternatively, a hip, two-measure ascending and descending line, which walks from the II (B7) chord in measure 9 to the V (E7) chord in measure 10 can be used instead, as shown. For good "measure," a walking turnaround line has been included in measures 11 (I) and 12 (V). **Performance Tip:** Begin each line with the middle finger, followed by the index, etc. The exceptions are measures 9, 10, and 12, which should start with the pinky.

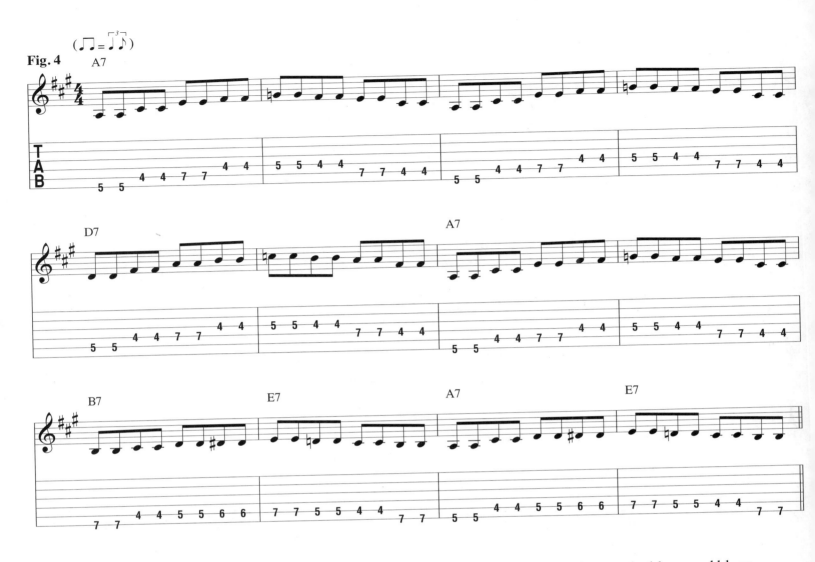

Fig. 5 is constructed around a dynamic octave jump that is popular in boogie woogie, blues, and blues-rock music. **Performance Tip:** Use the middle finger and pinky for the low and high octave notes, respectively, for all three chord changes, as this will put your hand in a proper position to handle the remaining notes in each phrase.

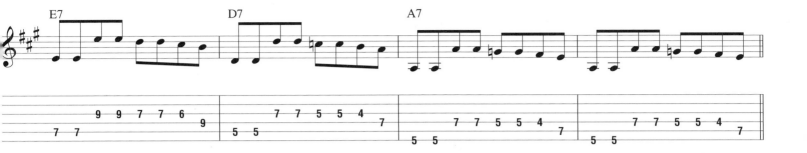

THE MAJOR PENTATONIC SCALE

Generally more upbeat and less bluesy than the Mixolydian mode due to the absence of the ♭7th degree, the major pentatonic scale, with just the root, 2nd, 3rd, 5th, and 6th, lies comfortably under the fingers while providing streamlined forward motion. Fig. 6 contains a recommended fingering in the key of A.

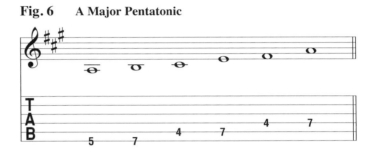

Fig. 6   A Major Pentatonic

In Fig. 7, observe how ending the one-measure phrase on the 3rd, relative to each chord change, makes for a seamless cycle of notes ascending and descending the scale. **Performance Tip:** Start each pattern with the middle finger.

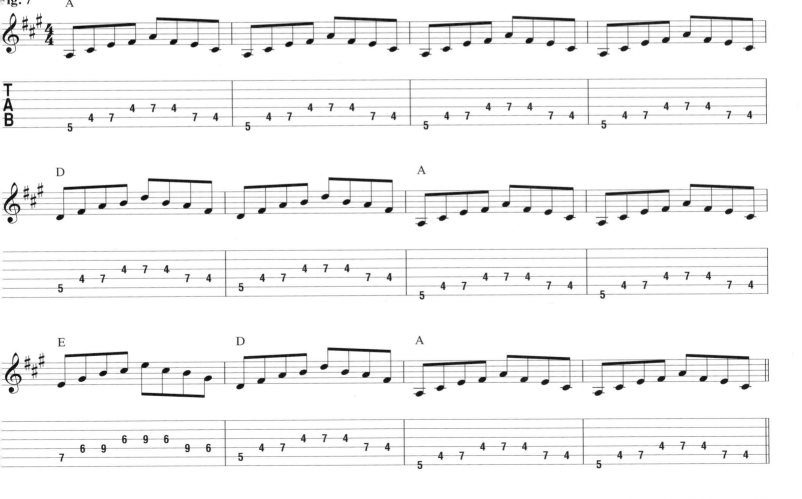

Fig. 8 does not "walk" as predictably as previous examples due to the doubled eighth-note root, 3rd, and 5th. The result is an added dollop of energy translating into additional forward motion. **Performance Tip:** The root, 3rd, and 5th notes of the major scale together form a major triad, hence the stable, consonant sound of the patterns.

Even more musical propulsion occurs in Fig. 9 due to the propensity of doubled eighth notes. **Performance Tip:** The turnaround to the V (E) chord in measure 12 "borrows" the 4th (D) from the Mixolydian mode and the ♭5th (E♭) from the blues scale in order to create a smooth, chromatic "string" of notes from the major 3rd (C♯) of the A chord up to the root (E) of the E chord.

At the breakneck tempos often occurring in boogie woogie music, quarter notes can also deliver potent drive, as Fig. 10 illustrates. See how only the root, 5th, and 6th notes are employed, as the absence of the tonality-defining major 3rd makes for a bit of ambiguity contributing to the sense of anticipation and forward motion. **Performance Tip:** As usual, start with the middle finger, followed by the index, pinky, and index fingers.

THE COMPOSITE BLUES SCALE

The best of both worlds appears in the composite blues scale, with select notes from the Mixolydian mode and the blues scale combined, as in Fig. 11. All things considered, it is the most useful boogie woogie scale, with the ♭3rd from the blues scale and the major 3rd and ♭7th from the Mixolydian mode included. Be aware how the scale is especially effective in the open-position "blues keys" of A (Fig. 12) and E (Fig. 13).

Fig. 11   A Composite Blues

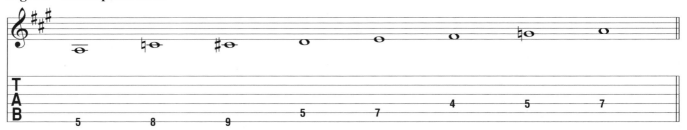

Fig. 12   A Composite Blues

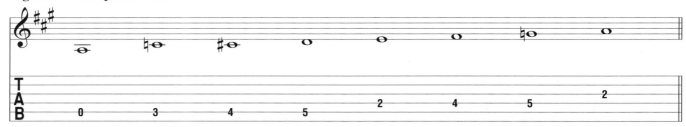

Fig. 13   E Composite Blues

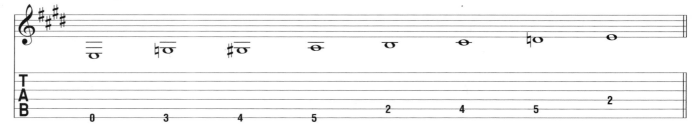

Fig. 14 is a classic "rolling" 12-bar cut-boogie progression. An advantage to the key of A, long known by sly blues and blues-rock guitarists, is the availability of open-string roots for each chord change, thereby precluding barre-chord positions if so desired. None other than the legendary Freddie King employed the pattern in the key of E for the I and IV chords in "Hide Away." **Performance Tip:** Alternate down and up pick strokes throughout for peak efficiency and the proper swing feel.

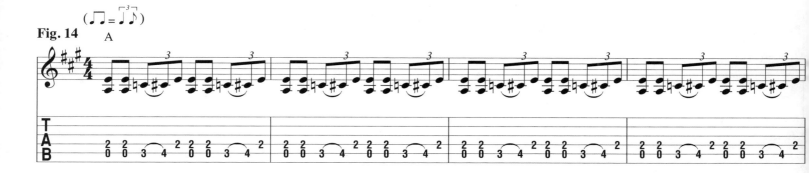

Fig. 14

As will continue to be seen, the blues-approved move from the ♭3rd (C) to the major 3rd (C♯) is a bedrock characteristic of boogie woogie music. Fig. 15 combines it with a descending move from the ♭7th (G) to the 6th (F♯), which encourages movement back to the root for the next measure. **Performance Tip:** Play the G and F♯ notes with the pinky and ring fingers, respectively.

The key of E requires some nimble finger work for the V (B) and possibly the IV (A) chord changes. Fig. 16 shows one typical solution to the musical "problem" of accessing the V chord. **Performance Tip:** Use the same fingering for the V chord as the IV chord after making the "leap" from fret 2 with the index finger to fret 5 with the middle finger, etc.

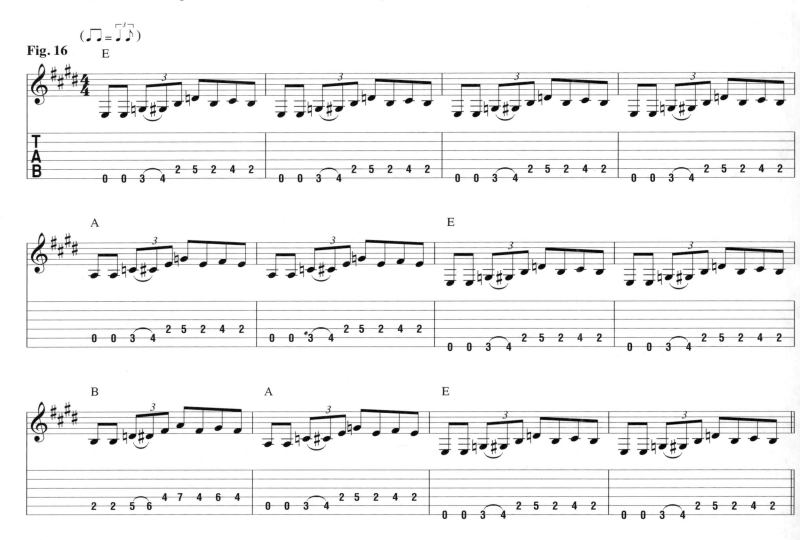

Like Fig. 4 in the Mixolydian mode section, Fig. 17 contains two-measure patterns instead of one-measure lines. As before, it presents intriguing options on how to deal with measures 9 and 10 of a 12-bar blues, which are usually arranged as V (B) and IV (A) chord changes. This time out, a two-measure V (B) chord pattern was chosen. **Performance Tip:** As all notes are swung eighths, alternate down and up pick strokes.

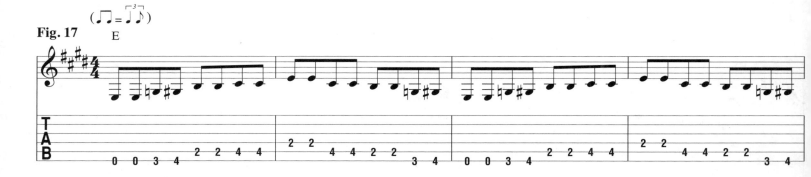

A stronger blues vibe casts its darker hue over Fig. 18 due to the increased emphasis on the ♭7th note, which appears on beat 3 of each chord change. **Performance Tip:** Access the ♭7 notes with the pinky.

Fig. 18

Fig. 19 takes a different tack than any of the other musical examples. The root notes are not contained in the patterns, and beat 1 of each change features the classic ♭3rd to 3rd blues move. Nonetheless, they provide a full harmony when played over a bass or other rhythm instrument supplying the root notes. **Performance Tip:** Utilize the middle and ring fingers for beat 1 of each measure.

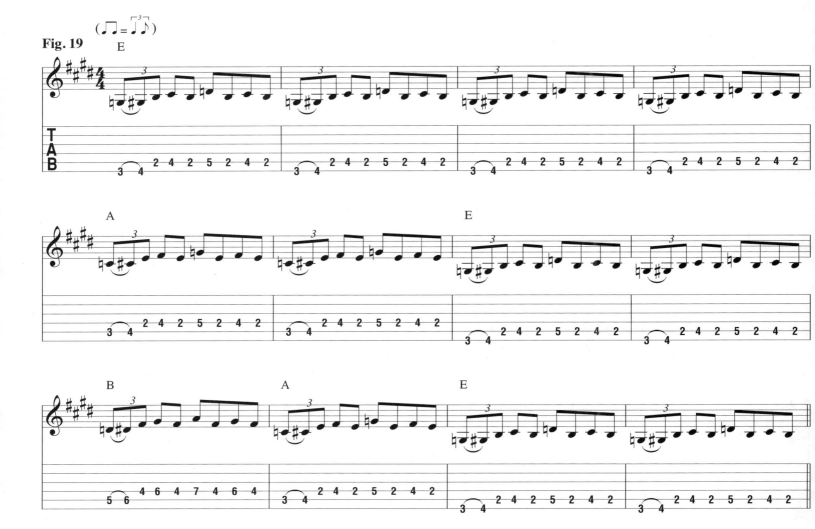

THE BLUES SCALE

Though consisting of just six notes, the blues scale in Fig. 20 is exceedingly versatile due to the inclusion of the ♭3rd and ♭7th "blues notes" like its close relative, the minor pentatonic scale (not shown), as well as the gritty ♭5th "blues note." Furthermore, its value is no mystery when one considers the other three notes are the root, 4th, and 5th—the essential foundation of blues, boogie woogie music, and their offshoots.

Fig. 20   A Blues Scale

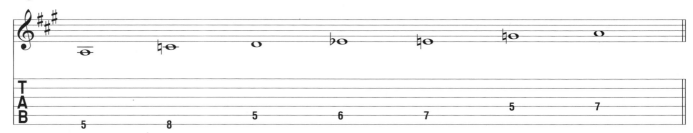

The single-note bass line in Fig. 21 is the essence of guitar boogie in the minds of many. Known popularly as the signature lick in ZZ Top's "La Grange" (1973), it contains chordal elements along with bass-string notes. Its genesis actually goes back to the landmark, early solo boogies of John Lee Hooker and confirms the enduring power of the minor pentatonic scale. **Performance Tip:** The picking pattern is especially critical to make it "boogie" with gusto. Play it: down–up–up–up–up–up–up–down–down. (**Note:** See Chapter 3 for an in-depth look at the primal blues artistry of John Lee Hooker.)

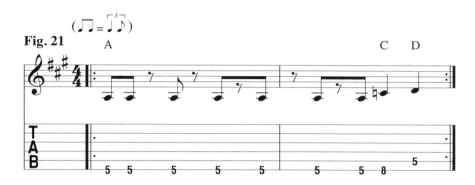

Fig. 22 contains the hip ♭5th (E♭) as a grace note preceding the 5th (E) and arriving at the ♭7th (G) in a striking display of blues power. **Performance Tip:** Use the middle and ring fingers, respectively, for the ♭5th-to-5th hammer-on maneuver.

Fig. 23 is a popular variation on Fig. 22 with the dynamic octave jump employed famously by Buddy Guy and others. A standard blues turnaround goes well with this pattern, though it could be inserted into any of the examples if so desired. **Performance Tip:** Alternating down and up pick strokes is recommended.

Fig. 24 is similar to "Green Onions" and theoretically in A minor rather than A major due to the emphasis on the ♭3rd relative to each chord change. In addition, with the absence of the ♭5th (E♭), it uses the minor pentatonic scale for all practical purposes. **Performance Tip:** Try picking "down–down–up–down–down–up," even though the last note changes strings by moving downward.

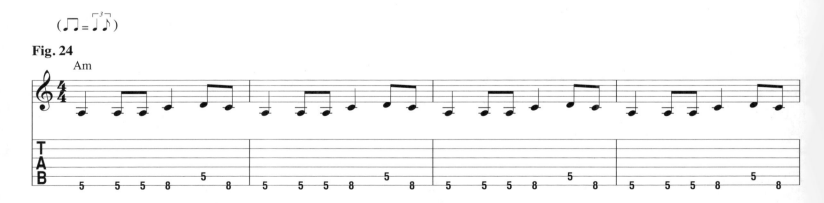

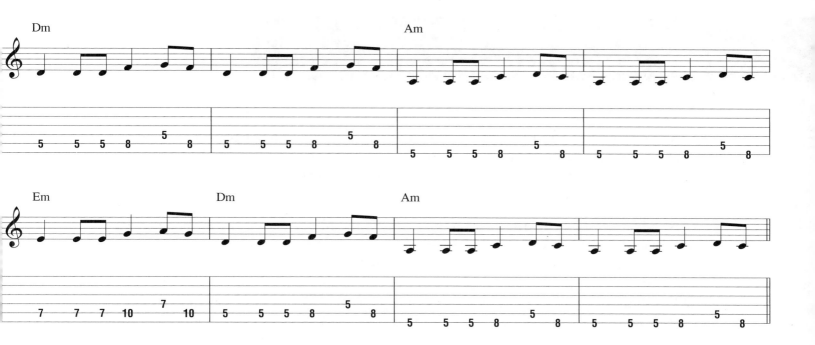

CHAPTER 2
DYADS RELATIVE TO THE I, IV, AND V CHORD CHANGES

Dyads, or double stops, are especially useful forms of harmony in boogie woogie guitar, as they can imply more musical weight than they actually contain and are easily moveable. They appear mostly as melodic 3rds and 6ths, though heavier 4ths and 5ths occasionally show up, too. Virtually without exception, the dyads change keys relative to the chords.

Classic blues and boogie harmonies propel Fig. 25. In order to accentuate the boogie beat, root bass notes have been inserted on the downbeats in between the 3rds, similarly to two-handed piano boogie woogie. Whenever possible, they should be included. Observe how they precede each measure on the "and" of beat 4 while also anticipating the next new chord change as in measures 4, 6, 8, 9, and 10. The addition of a turnaround is always an option and works well with this particular pattern. **Performance Tip:** Though this type of riff is best handled fingerstyle (thumb for bass notes and fingers for the dyads), it's recommended you pick down on the bass notes and up on the dyads for maximum swing if using a pick.

Fig. 25

Fig. 26 is a Mixolydian mode variation on Fig. 23. Be aware that there are others derived from different scales. A turnaround seems appropriate to the progression. **Performance Tip:** Use the ring and middle fingers, low to high, for the first two dyads in each measure. Use the ring and index fingers, low to high, for the third dyad. In measure 11, anchor the index finger on string 4 at fret 5 and descend on string 5 with the pinky, ring, and middle fingers. Barre G/D on beat 1 of measure 12 with the index finger.

The fertile fields of the Mixolydian mode are harvested once again in Fig. 27. This time the dyads in 3rds are played as broken chords, creating a sinewy, swinging shuffle groove. **Performance Tip:** As often is the case, alternating down and up pick strokes is strongly encouraged.

Dyads in 6ths are less common than 3rds in guitar boogie woogie but have their place nonetheless, as demonstrated in Fig. 28. Observe the way the V (E) and IV (D) patterns in measures 9 and 10, respectively, do not follow the parallel forms of the I (A) and IV chords in measures 1–4 and 5–6, respectively. As an unspoken rule of blues and boogie woogie music, it is imperative to not overly rely on predictable parallel chordal forms. **Performance Tip:** For the cleanest sound, employ hybrid picking when playing 6ths.

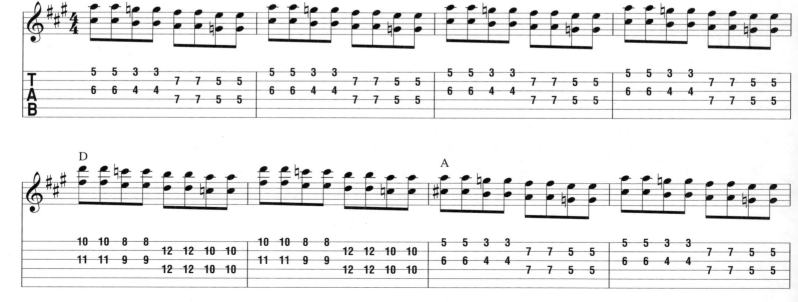

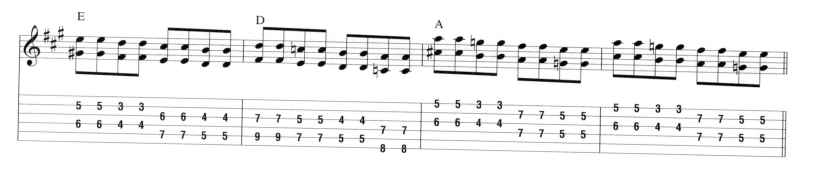

Fig. 29 contains an unusual, but hip, pattern combining 3rds, 4ths, ♭5ths, and 5ths in a smooth, chromatic sequence for a welcome change of sound from the ubiquitous Mixolydian mode. Not the least of its attributes is the gnarly ♭5th on beat 3, which adds even more musical tension than the ♭3rd.
Performance Tip: Anchor the middle finger on the root note of each change while walking up with the index, ring, pinky, and pinky fingers.

CHAPTER 3
JOHN LEE HOOKER AND SOLO GUITAR BOOGIE ACCOMPANIMENT

Guitar cut-boogie patterns did not begin with Hooker, and indeed, he rarely ever recorded any examples. However, his countless variations on the I-chord boogie, especially those where he plays solo, accompanied only by his stomping feet, are essential listening for the understanding of his technique as follows. Clearly, they did not call him "The Boogie Man" for nothing!

(**Note:** Though Hooker played almost exclusively in open tunings such as A and G and often with a capo, the musical figures will all be in standard tuning for the easiest access to his style and to be consistent with the rest of the book. In addition, while he played with bare fingers, they may be played with a combination of pick and fingers, as Chapter 5 will deal with fingerstyle boogie.)

Fig. 30 is similar to the "birth of the boogie" as envisioned by Hooker. Remember: the rhythm is everything! Make it snap and crackle. **Performance Tip:** After picking the B note with a down stroke and hammering to the C and C♯ notes with the middle and ring fingers, respectively, follow with "down–up–down–up" strokes.

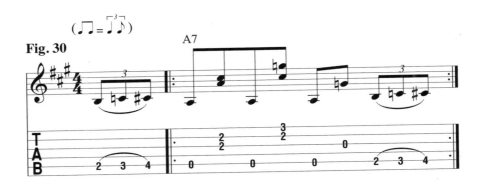

Though most Hooker boogies are medium to fast, he composed slow, insinuating classics, too. Fig. 31 "crawls" like a "snake," adding menace with the contrasting A7 voicing and the blues scale bass riff featuring the nasty ♭3rd (C).

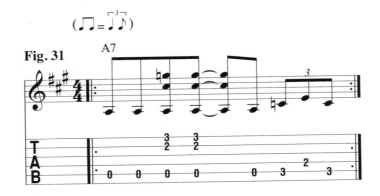

Fig. 32 contains A major and A7 voicings in a classic move guaranteed to provide extra propulsion. Contributing even more momentum and swing are the last two upbeats on the A7 and A chords.

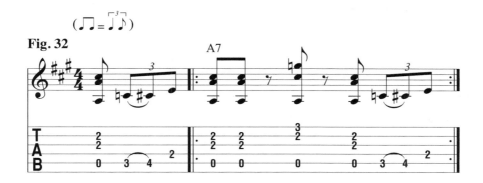

A change in harmony from A to an implied C chord occurs in Fig. 33. Indeed, the bass notes on beat 4 could also be seen to imply movement from C to D. **Performance Tip:** Play the notes on string 5 with the pick and pluck strings 3 and 2 with the middle and ring fingers, respectively.

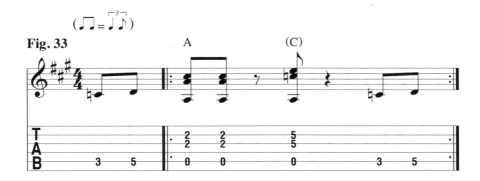

A rare change of key to D gives Fig. 34 a much different sound. Be aware that Hooker was in an open tuning and capoed, but as previously stated, playing in standard tuning makes the patterns more accessible and useful.

Fig. 35 could be seen to suggest a chord change from G7 to Gm, but most blues musicians would hear it all as in G major or implied G7. Nonetheless, the important effect is of musical tension being created and then released in the span of one measure—an important consideration in I-chord boogie music. **Performance Tip:** Play the D and F notes with the ring and index fingers, respectively, followed by the ring, index, pinky, and index fingers for the descending bass-strings run.

Due to his lack of tuning to concert pitch—or more likely the result of capoing at fret 1 in open A tuning—Hooker on occasion played in B♭, as seen in Fig. 36. Regardless of the reason, it presents a welcome opportunity to boogie in a key away from the usual suspects (E, A, and G) and presents a bit of a fingering challenge. Similar to Fig. 35, the forward motion moves from anticipation to resolution. **Performance Tip:** Play the 3rds on beats 1–3 with (low to high) ring and index, middle and index, and middle and index.

JOHN LEE HOOKER INTERVIEW

Miles Davis once commented to John Lee Hooker, "Man, you are so funky you are up to your neck in mud." No scant praise from a bonafide hipster and patriarch of cool. Along with Charlie Patton, Muddy Waters, and Howlin' Wolf, Hooker occupies that vaunted space where personal expression and artistic achievement in the blues meet to make a lasting, profound statement on the human condition. As opposed to his esteemed peers, however, his music is so startlingly original as to be without precedent. His monochord boogie and blues numbers contain his magnificent bass growl and clanging guitar combined with his stomping feet to create hypnotic, monumental music. In a genre where the rough edges of the solo country blues form were gradually ground off to fit the requirements of ensemble playing, he only made cursory adjustments, counting on his sidemen to have "big ears" and follow his intuitive chord changes.

I conducted this interview for *Guitar One* magazine in January, 2001 in the San Jose home of JLH.

What kind of music were people playing in the clubs when you went to Detroit?

Blues.

You played solo at first?

Um-hmm, yes, just me. (Laughs) I played my electric guitar and tapped my foot. Later on, I played with small bands—two and three pieces.

Were there others performing solo at that time?

No, just me. I was the biggest thing that was happening in the nightclubs. You know, I wish we could have those days again, but I don't think they will come back. I enjoyed those days, sitting and playing guitar and talking to people. Now I can't do that. But those were the good old days.

In 1990, I saw you perform solo at the Chicago Blues Festival.

Yeah, I remember that very well. The blues I can't forget because I did it for a good many years.

Did you ever play slide?

Nah, I never did anything that big with it. My cousin Earl (Ed: Earl Hooker) played it really, really good.

Many people think Earl was maybe the best guitarist in Chicago.

He was the best! (Laughs) He could make the guitar talk like a human being with the wah wah.

Did you two ever play together?

Yeah. I had my band, and he had his band, and we would go out on the road together.

You mention Henry's Swing Club on Hastings Street in Detroit in several of your songs. Do you remember the first time you went there?

Actually, it was on Madison Street in the early '40s. I was walking down Hastings Street, though, and heard the natural born boogie out on the sidewalk in front of a club, so I dropped in there one night. But, oh yeah, I have a lot of memories of Henry's Swing Club. Then I wrote "Boogie Chillen," and it was a big hit. Everybody was talking about it. A lot of rock 'n' roll has that beat.

Where did you get the "boogie beat"?

I got it from my stepfather, Will Moore. He married my mother after she and my real father broke up. When I was young, a guitar player named Tony Hollins used to come around to see my sister Alice. He had recorded some and he was a barber in Chicago. He had an old Silvertone guitar that he gave me. My father let me keep it, but I could not bring it in the house. He was a minister, and I couldn't play blues in his house. He was a preacher and he didn't allow it. But, Will Moore was a guitar player, and he would do that beat (sings a cut-boogie rhythm).

Do you know where he got it?

I don't know, but he got it from way back. I know that he learned some things from Charlie Patton. I met Charlie Patton through my stepfather. They sounded so good. I never saw Blind Lemon Jefferson, though, when he came through Mississippi.

Do you think the blues has changed over the years?

Umm-hmm. They're much deeper. There used to be blues from the cotton fields, the lonesome blues. Now they're from the city.

Do the blues get deeper the longer you play them?

Depends on the person. I know mine did. My blues were deep from the start.

Do you ever listen to your old records?

All the time.

Which are your favorites?

"In the Mood," "Boogie Chillen," "Dimples."

Do you like the old songs better, where you are playing solo?

Yeah, because there's more me. (Laughs)

Which guitars are you playing the most lately?

Gibsons (Ed: ES-335). I have been playing them for years. They give them to me.

They should. People see you playing them and then they want one, too.

Yeah, I know and Gibson knows it, too. (Laughs)

Other people do not sound like you when they play the same guitar, however.

No, they don't. (Laughs) Nobody like John Lee Hooker. They try, but they can't. I admire them trying, though.

You are playing a lot more guitar these days.

I always could… but I didn't while I was doing more singing. I'm playing more now, and it's some great blues.

You have made quite a few albums with other musicians as guest artists. Is there anyone else whom you would like to record with?

He played with John Mayall, who had so many people in his band. He quit for a long, long time, but now he's back playing again. Peter Green. Great player, woo, yeah. He said he wanted to and I would like him to play on my next record.

Green just made a record of Robert Johnson's songs. Did you ever see Johnson in person?

I never did, but I always wanted to. I heard some of his records. He was good—he had a different style. Yeah, Robert Johnson. He was born in Mississippi, too.

Guitar players always want to hear about Jimi Hendrix.

They sure do. Me, too. I loved him, but I never met him.

He was a big fan of yours.

I understand that. He was a great guitarist. He could play the hard blues, rock, and blues. He could do both. Whatever, he could do it all. He was a young man when he died. Too young. Drugs. I lived in New York in the '60s on Bleecker Street when he was there but never did meet him. There was a lot of music going on then and a lot of nice girls. Bob Dylan came to see me play once at Gerdes Folk City on West 4th Street, and I put him on the bandstand. He sang a few songs and stayed at the hotel I was in. He sang the blues early on in his career.

Do you think Dylan is a blues man?

Woo, yeah, he's a blues man.

Do you still enjoy playing after all these years?

Yes, I do, after all these years. I'll be playing until I'm gone. I may retire from the road, but I'll still play here and there. It gives me joy. It's my life. (Ed: John Lee Hooker left us on June 21, 2001.)

CHAPTER 4
ROCKIN' THE BOOGIE

Rock guitarists have typically taken boogie riffs and patterns and pumped them up with energy, often at faster tempos. Notice the way the ♭3rd note or ♭III chord appears consistently.

Fig. 37 is a choice example, where the I chord from Fig. 14 is altered with the addition of an alternating bass lick on string 6, thereby combining notes from the blues scale and the Mixolydian mode for a richer, fuller sound. **Performance Tip:** Anchor the index finger on string 4 at fret 2 and execute both hammer-ons with the middle and ring fingers. Additionally, alternate pick strokes, beginning with a downstroke.

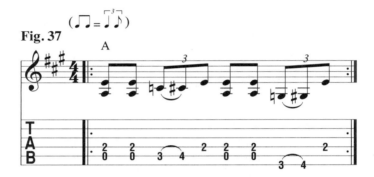

Fig. 38 shows a typical cut-boogie pattern altered rhythmically to straight eighth notes for a more driving effect. Foghat, the great British blues and boogie band, employed a similar pattern for their epic, erotic "Slow Ride." **Performance Tip:** Pick "down–up–up–up–down–up."

Jimmy Page created a somewhat similar pattern, shown in Fig. 39, for his anthemic "Rock and Roll." **Performance Tip:** Employ alternate pick strokes, including for the individual notes on beat 2, in order to maintain a consistent rhythmic flow.

Fig. 40 contains an unusual I–IV move within the span of a measure. Though it may sound reminiscent of "In the Midnight Hour" and "Lady Madonna," the utilization of the classic ♭3rd–3rd bass-string embellishment for both chord changes places it firmly in the boogie and blues camp. **Performance Tip:** Alternate pick strokes.

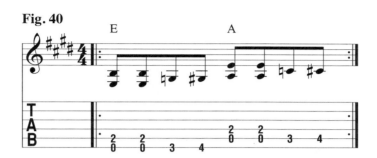

Fig. 41 has a dark, menacing feel going back to John Lee Hooker and is often favored by heavy blues-rockers. The dramatic E (I)–A (IV)–G (♭III) sequence is a classic of the genre. **Performance Tip:** Alternate pick strokes, please.

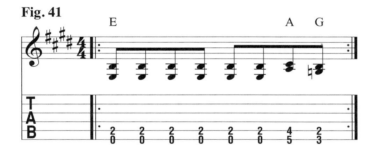

Fig. 42 shows how the envelope may be pushed from boogie and blues to rock in order to create a big-beat chordal pattern. "I'm Cryin'" by the Animals features a similar sequence. **Performance Tip:** Try all downstrokes for maximum punch.

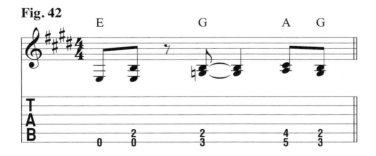

Minor-key boogies exist, but they are few and far between. Fig. 43 is similar to the Sonny Boy Williamson II song "Help Me" and Muddy Waters' "Trouble No More," blurring the line between blues and boogie, as often occurs. **Performance Tip:** After barring for the Am chord, use the index finger as a small barre for the C triad and the ring finger for the D triad while maintaining the fret 5 hand position.

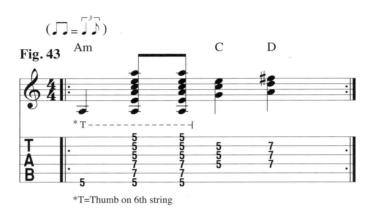

Confirming the ubiquity of the boogie beat, none other than the Who utilized a chord pattern similar to Fig. 44 in their live version of "Amazing Journey" from *Tommy*. Though it does not include the ♭III chord, but instead uses common I, IV, and V changes, the rhythm is indeed an outgrowth of boogie woogie. **Performance Tip:** Strum "down–up–down–up–up–down–up."

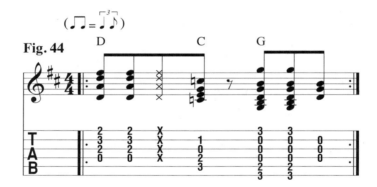

Fig. 45 takes the boogie concept to perhaps its logical conclusion in rock with a classic I–♭III–IV progression. **Performance Tip:** Barre strings 2 and 1 with the pinky for the "voodoo" E7♯9 chord. Leave the pinky on the G note on string 1 and finger the G chord with your (low to high) ring and pinky fingers.

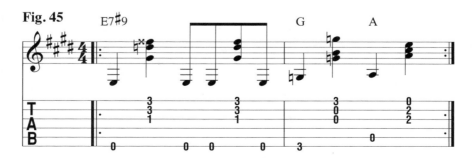

CHAPTER 5
IMPROVISING GUITAR BOOGIE

Solo guitar in any musical genre can be a formidable technical challenge, especially when compared to two-handed piano playing on the "88s." However, the rewards of learning to play solo boogie woogie guitar are manifold. If nothing else, the resultant chops from maintaining the driving beat will positively impact all your playing. More importantly, the options of creating some combination of moving bass lines, chords, and melodies leading to improvisation is an accomplishment affording great musical satisfaction. Be aware how all the figures are moveable unless otherwise noted. **Performance Tip:** Fingerstyle picking is highly recommended for efficiency and to better produce the swing rhythms. That said, for selected patterns, flat picking or, better yet, hybrid picking will also suffice.

The 12-bar progression in Fig. 46 introduces the concept of walking bass lines in conjunction with chord forms. Check out measures 9–10, where the implied harmony moves ii (Dm)–V (G), instead of the more conventional V (G)–IV (F), via a cool harmonized bass line in 3rds. In addition, observe the "passing notes" on beat 4 of measure 9, which are skipped on the way back down in measure 10 in typical II–V walking bass line fashion. **Performance Tip:** Use the thumb of your right hand for the walking bass lines and the index finger picking upward in counterpoint for the chordal elements.

Fig. 47 shows a most compact way to access dominant voicings and the classic ♭3rd–3rd move in a cut-boogie progression. It would make a great "head" to be followed by a walking pattern.

Fig. 48 lays out a boogie accompaniment that will be followed in Fig. 49 with the same patterns combined with improvised licks. **Performance Tip:** Finger the swung bass notes on beat 1 of each measure with the thumb. This will leave your hand in a more advantageous position to access the dyads.

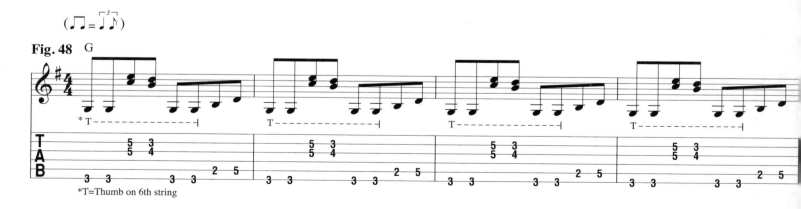

*T=Thumb on 6th string

Fig. 49 contains one of the most effective methods for improvising within a boogie woogie or 12-bar blues progression: alternate measures of accompaniment with improvised measures relative to the chord changes. Dyads in 3rds phrased as triplets provide harmonic weight and momentum, though carefully selected single-note lines are likewise intelligent choices. **Performance Tip:** Always observe the cardinal rule when engaging in "call and response": maintain or strongly imply the shuffle rhythm throughout.

With a nod towards the lauded "Boogie Man," Fig. 50 takes the basic concept of mixing root bass notes in dynamic contrast with dyads identifying the chord changes and produces a stomping progression. **Performance Tip:** This progression is not moveable. It makes a tough argument for picking fingerstyle, with the thumb thumping down on the bass strings and the index finger picking upward on the dyads.

Fig. 51 is the improvised version of Fig. 50. As seen in Fig. 49, triplets are one of the best improvisational tools to keep the momentum moving forward in solo boogie woogie guitar. In addition, they flow smoothly and dynamically from the swung eighth notes that begin each improvised measure. **Performance Tip:** Finger the B chord in measure 9 with the middle and ring fingers, low to high. In measure 10, play the dyad with the ring and index fingers, low to high.

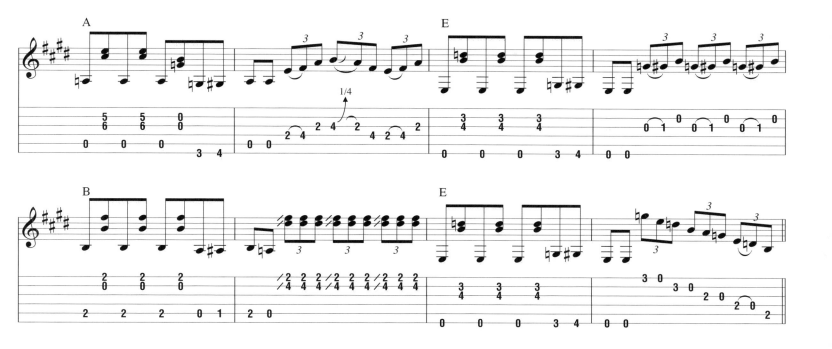

Ready for a toe-tapper? Fig. 52 should be taken at a gallop. The straight-ahead "four-on-the-floor" rhythm is reflected in the improvisation measures, too, though the deliberate placement of the eighth notes adds phrasing variety. **Performance Tip:** "Walk" the accompanying major pentatonic bass lines with the middle, index, pinky, and index fingers.

Fig. 52

Adding to the challenge of solo boogie guitar improvising is when the "progression" consists solely of the hypnotic repetition of the I chord. The absence of a moving harmony means the rhythm has to have a deep, unwavering groove, and the licks have to complement and enhance the accompaniment. Fig. 53 bears a passing resemblance to "Parachute Woman" and "Roadhouse Blues" in rhythmic feel, but with the crucial difference being the alternating improvised measures. **Performance Tip:** Play the G and E notes in the accompanying measures with the middle and index fingers, respectively.

Fig. 54 contains walking bass lines and dyads in a driving shuffle progression that will allow for creative improvisational opportunities. Check out measures 9–10, which move harmonically with the hipper II (B)–V (E) rather than V (B)–IV (A) changes. **Performance Tip:** The left-hand fingerings are critical and a bit unorthodox to boot, with all five digits joining in the action. The bass lines in measures 1, 3, 5, 7, and 11 require the thumb, index, pinky, and index. Measures 2, 4, 6 and 8 utilize the index, index, pinky, and index. Measures 9–10 work best with the pinky, index, index, pinky, pinky, index, index, and pinky. Access the dyads with the ring and middle fingers, low to high. Use the thumb (bass strings) and index (dyads) to power your right hand "rhythm machine."

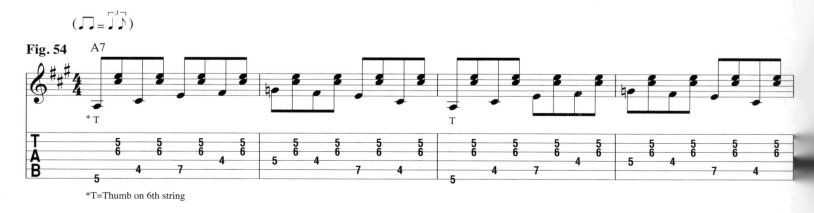

*T=Thumb on 6th string

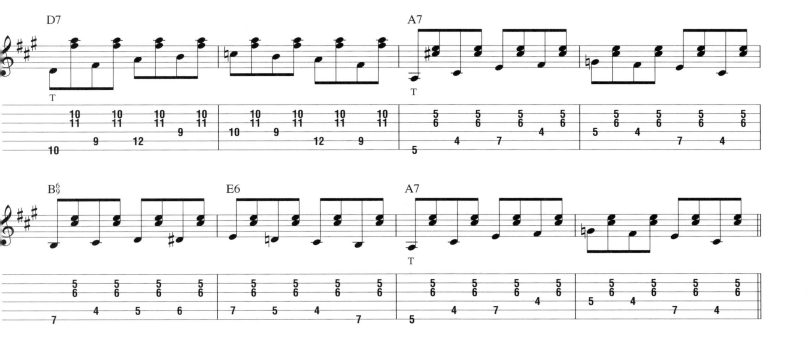

Fig. 55 is the improvisational version of Fig. 54. Two punchy licks on beats 2 and 4 per improvised measure, derived from the composite blues scale (Mixolydian mode plus blues scale) relative to each chord change in swung eighth notes or triplets, flow organically from the accompaniment patterns.

Performance Tip: Play the bass notes in the improvised measures with the left-hand thumb.

*T=Thumb on 6th string

One-beat improvised licks also appear in Fig. 56, but only on beat 4 of each measure, save for measure 12 in the turnaround. Keep in mind that they do not have to be fret-bending displays of virtuosity, but need to feel logically generated from the accompaniment while still making a melodic statement. Like Fig. 55, a steady, propulsive groove is the ultimate goal. **Performance Tip:** All measures, except 2, 4, and 12, contain licks that are to be played off the index-finger barre.

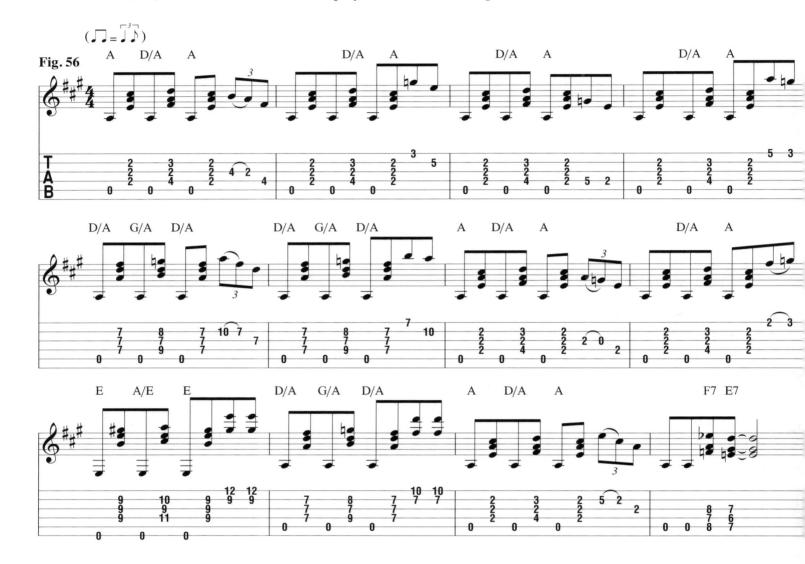

Fig. 57 likewise features one-beat licks on beat 4, but in conjunction with cut-boogie patterns. Notice how the licks are all phrased as triplets to complement the swing bass lines. Additionally, II (F♯)–V (B) changes voiced as 5ths appear in measures 9–10 as optional harmony and a change of pace. **Performance Tip:** A flatpick could be employed if for no other reason than it would be a good right-hand exercise.

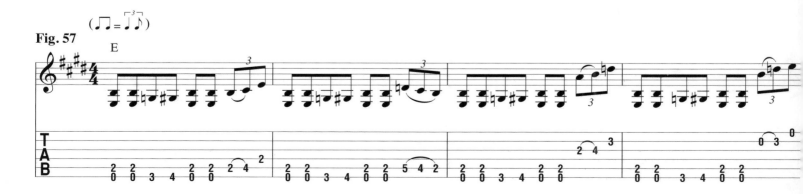

By alternating full measures of blues licks with cut-boogie patterns, Fig. 58 allows the greatest freedom to improvise. Again, it cannot be stressed enough how critical it is to try and create rhythmically propulsive licks that flow seamlessly from the cut-boogie measures. In addition, check out the V (B7) and IV (A7) chords in measures 9 and 10, respectively, employing similar ascending "turnaround patterns" in contrast to measures 1–8 while also goosing the momentum forward to the actual turnaround in measures 11–12.

Performance Tip: Play the pair of A notes on beat 1 of measure 10 with the middle finger, thereby putting the hand in fine position to begin the ascending pattern with the index finger on string 5, followed by the middle and ring fingers. Conversely, use the pinky for the E note on fret 7 of string 5 in measure 11. Next, walk up string 6 with the index, middle, and ring fingers while leaving the pinky in place through beat 1 of measure 12. Arrive at beat 1 in measure 12 with the ring finger on string 6.

*T=Thumb on 6th string

Fig. 59 takes liberties with the usual Mixolydian mode and major pentatonic walking lines by utilizing a dramatic, ascending, chromatic line from the 6th following the I (G7), IV (C7), and V (D7) triple-stop chords on beat 1 of measures 1, 3, 5, 7, and 11. The result is nimble, swinging drive and forward motion. Be sure to see how the boogie pattern in measure 9 deviates from the others in order to flow more smoothly into the improvisation in measure 10. **Performance Tip:** Walk up from the open strings in measures 1, 3, 5, 7, and 11 with the index and middle fingers, arriving at the tonic note in measures 2, 4, 6, 8, and 12 with the ring finger in preparation for the improvisation.

SELECT DISCOGRAPHY

JOHN LEE HOOKER

Detroit 1948–1949 (Atlantic/Savoy 92910-2)

Alone (2-CD Tomato 2696602)

The Best of John Lee Hooker (Suite Beat/VeeJay SBCD 2012)

ARTHUR "GUITAR BOOGIE" SMITH

Here Comes the Boogie Man (Jasmine JASMCD 3502)

One Good Boogie Deserves Another (Jasmine JASMCD 3521)

DR. ROSS

Boogie Disease (Arhoolie CD 371)

CANNED HEAT

Hooker 'n Heat (Liberty/Electra)

Living the Blues (Liberty)

JIMMY BRYANT

Stratosphere Boogie: The Flaming Guitars of Jimmy Bryant and Speedy West (Razor & Tie)

JOE MAPHIS

Fire on the Strings (101 Distribution)

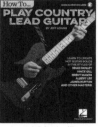
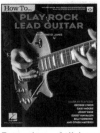
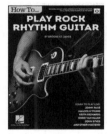
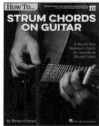